TIME
OF THE
ICEBERGS
POEMS
BY
DAVID
EGGLETON

OTAGO

Much of *Time of the Icebergs* was written while David Eggleton, a performance poet and writer who grew up between Fiji and New Zealand, was a Writer-in-Residence at the Michael King Writers Centre in Auckland in 2009. Eggleton's many awards include six times Book Reviewer of the Year in the Montana New Zealand Book Awards, PEN Best First Book of Poetry in 1987, the Robert Burns Fellowship and, uniquely among New Zealand poets, he was London *Time Out*'s Street Entertainer of the Year in 1985. He has also written or contributed to many books on the arts in New Zealand, and has produced several documentaries, CDs and short films.

Published by Otago University Press
Level 1, 398 Cumberland Street
PO Box 56 Dunedin
New Zealand
Fax: 64 3 479 8385
Email: university.press@otago.ac.nz
www.otago.ac.nz/press

ISBN 978 1 877578 02 1

Published with the assistance of Creative New Zealand
Typeset in Garamond by Otago University Press
Printed in New Zealand by PrintStop Ltd, Wellington

Contents

Birds

Flock
at sunset,
message flung skywards,
shreds
into the dark
alphabet.

Time of the Icebergs

In the time of the icebergs –
big black baby buggies pushed by women
in hoodies, denim and eff-off boots.
Crop circles on Google Earth say NO to Monsanto.
Boxy four-wheel-drives plane through the wet –
semi-amphibious barges, growling up and down,
piloted by yummy mummies, or tattooed property
developers in cargo shorts, their tee-shirts
emblazoned with Crowded House logos,
their capitalist warrior chariots splashing kerbs.
Buses pull out wheezing, puffing exhaust,
loaded to the gunnels with glaze-eyed tourists –
destination, *Bliss or Damnation.*

Glossolalia of the Undie 500 clown cars;
smashed glass of the student quarter glimmery as jewels;
detritus of bonfires blown hither and yon,
the shouty mouthy denizens of bouncy Castle Street
wandering in fellowship of the sofa burns
to the great forcing apparatus university,
glowing with self-declared enlightenment;
and death by chocolate beckons,
from Cadbury's vast lakes of cocoa butter,
to vulgarians who flog heritage buildings for parking.
Bringing frost, a flotilla of white blocks;
winter bloom of blue muffin-tops over low-slung jeans,
and gales in the face which smack like wet fish;
chill fingerbones that touch you from far away,
in the time of the icebergs.

The city at night one vast monastery
under holy hush of snow;
and bent beneath their hoods they go,
like capuchin monks praying in cloisters,
Ngati Cappuccino or Ngati Bogan,
eye-sockets deep pits in snoods:
glaze-eyed jaded ones,
monkish, cowling the head for respect,
or to recapture the rapture;
and a hooded phantom runs,
breathing out steam,
a warrior monk who travels light.
Closer, you see her face,
ethereal as that of a novice nun,
beneath her hoodie,
in the time of the icebergs.

Warming

Up here,
seagulls float like kites on thermals.
Down there,
a car canters like a racehorse
through pasture, towards Aramoana.
The giant wharf cranes of Port Chalmers
stand like steel giraffes in a story book,
and time is reluctant to turn the page.

A fishing boat's wake is
carving a V
in the freckled salty skin of the sea,
furrowing its calm green translucence,
until the sun squeezes juice from quarter
of a lemon onto the veiling, foam-white,
dissolved wings of a billion butterflies.
Pick up that foam, pick it up and drape it
across the dry riverbeds of the skies.

Driverless Ute

Mist in fine sunlight, salting spray away;
cupboards of cliffs, cracked and chipped;
shadows cannot open clouds, but trail their tumble
over waves strait-laced in pews;
an outboard's hard yakka under headland;
keen dolphins sky-larking and racing
just beneath the surface of the mind;
as learnt by heart these contours,
the dark birthmarks of islands,
catch the sun, steadily revealing
corrugated tracks stepping up grass
to the farm, the hills, the Maoritanga, the town,
all bundled together with number eight wire,
and dumped on the tray of a driverless ute,
revved up on the last of the petrol,
and spluttery, like water tanks drained
in late summer, leaving the taste of grinding
peppermill dust and dry forest floor.

On Beauty

You, scarred wahine, lift pounamu profile,
wearing a cap of plumed indignation:

leaf tannins of creeks rush across your tongue;
smoke from burn-offs wreathes your sensual

undulation, pelvic girdle of volcanoes,
forest mists – your rivers that midges sing.

By katipo's kiss, shimmering black and silver,
we're held, but in an embrace distant and hard:

your whenua yearns to tides and moon's glow.
Matrixed with ferns, your surf's tow rips under,

as Anzac horses might, on war monuments, prance.
Gales through mountain rifts moan your praises.

Between deep fiords: landslips of slow footsteps.
Lakes dark eyes, you triumph in your screen test.

Visions of Michael Joseph Savage

Old centennial parades gather forest weight,
roll out settler floats, as dream code talkers
once climbed from migrant ships, their mouths
spawning a God who cracked open earth and ate.
The land rush was thunder cracking open heads
of the tapu; tracts were slipped into ledgers of debt:
cargo cult pinnacles of a small green archipelago.

Diggers humped swags; prospectors rode horseback;
dairy herds tarantella'd through the Taranaki gate.
Now it's pig-stick martyrs in tartan bush-shirts;
axe-masters nailing light that nicks chain-saws;
tv show homesteaders who can communicate.

Taste of gumboot tea; sounds of coconut wireless;
baches bodged and poozled out of iceblock sticks;
enough pine trees to keep the Japanese in chopsticks.
Savage didn't foretell it, but to contemplate
his photo over a dozen stubbies is not to glimpse
a glorified mickey-taker smiling like the Pope,
but rather – not seen since Seddon – a visionary.

Pioneer hands, squeezing bagpipes of udders,
or streaked by greasy wool lanolins, helped hinge (on
pintles) gates to the nation, while *ladies bring a plate*
was phased out by nouveau kiwifruit chefs
garnishing cuisines of orange roughy with saffron.

January used to be dry, with soft, threshing grass;
across sunny canvas, chestnuts from shanghais flew;
lofty attitudes by windy platitudes were marked.
Each mountain then, an altar-table uplifted
over half-pints of school milk in a metal crate.

Those out took it on the chin; and embarrassment
was too many tea coupons, or else butterpats,
as, in honeyed memories of summer limbs,
one lolled or gambolled, followed a calling,
threw a sickie, or teased a go-kart into life,
watched a stubby Bristol Freighter carry its weight:
all the believers who sailed in Captain Cook's wake.

Now mellow whisky drinkers charge glasses;
now a free-range chill wind blows above
the high tide margin of seabed and foreshore,
beachside's whip-crack towel and spilled lotion.
Codgers praise *New Happyland* with cries of: oh, mate!
Yes, Pukeko clowns troop in, upstage the Kea Party.
So korero Maori to the tamariki, to the kids,
to the hundred alpine kiwi calling by moonlight.
And a hoha to the iwi by the fireside, the beacons.
When the pounamu harvest that's in flax baskets bulges,
a kapa haka for colonial warhorses led to their fate.

The Five Cent Coin

A puddle of silver makes a tumbled host of tuatara,
spun on wooden counters, dropped five cent coin.

Whence the hikipene, tickapenny, for soap, candles,
matches, for the paper, the milk, dropped five cent coin?

When the whole world was the size of a gobstopper
summoned with a rap on a glass top, dropped five cent coin.

Once it carried decimal weight and heft, handed down
from sovereigns and crowns, dropped five cent coin.

Bob, copper, ding, electrum, shiner, tanner, zack:
passed on, pocket to pocket, dropped five cent coin.

Legal tender, put it where your mouth is, accounts
due burn holes in pay packets, dropped five cent coin.

It filled a gap, that shiny dot, pitched or tossed acrobat,
stuck to the pavement by chuddy, dropped five cent coin.

Empty husk, a tiddlywink flicked to the end of the line,
the breeze light on sun-crinkled water, dropped five cent coin.

Escaping to roll, wobble, travel into corners, spiral
once or twice, fall face down, dropped five cent coin.

And still you see it here and there, in dust, or else gathered
and crammed into a jar for buttons, dropped five cent coin.

Graveyard School

Harpoon spires, coal smoke, iron rustbucket,
daylight's bright fine gold, cranny of the South.
Judgement's dungeon cell, lost hospital maze,
tiny ark with cabinets of curiosities padlocked.
The lone piper able to bring the young running
the nexus of street veins to the octagonal heart.
Then submarine arcades, fleets of wooden shops,
sell-out sermons on oyster saloons ready to open.

But between pipe skirls and wool skeins stands a
boil-in-the-bag city, whose teaspoon-tinkle stanzas
announce fine china cups are running over absently,
populace gone in search of oats and possum stew.
Who'll buy clay chamberpots, a weighing machine?
If buildings are porridge-coloured, eminent stone,
go down into the catacombs: there the dead snore.
The gannet colony's a rest home, sounding out oracles.

Repeat the series of thirty-nine steps after Cargill,
from his named summit, street, monument, corner,
and watch last Century wash up in cinema lacework.
Ironmonger's nails swapped for a sack of earth that's
sewn into a uniform riding through Canongate.
Under a shirt of frosty stars, the kilted hills.
An eight-sided poem spiders the crystal screen:
hail to the ears, the whole town gets up and cheers.

Ode to the Beercrate

Beercrate, part of landscape,
part of folklore memory,
staple of nostalgia.
Spartan, pragmatic, transient, expendable;
low-cost, mass-produced, abundantly social.
Assemblage knocked together
out of a few short pine slats with nails,
sometimes with a logo stencilled;
used by breweries as a container for holding glass bottles,
simple, almost elemental, totemic box, airy crate.
Stacked at the back of a pub in storage;
resembling street junk, mute but everpresent.
Unlabelled, stacked wooden pyramid,
fragile, yet enduring.
Block-like grid of horizontals and verticals,
bearing resemblance to state houses of the 1940s,
which is fitting because they celebrate the egalitarian ethos.

Put to the purpose for which they were made,
heavy clinking crates that symbolise plenty,
initiation, a necessary
part of hangi or wedding or barbecue.
Full of bottles, boozebarn accessories, macho,
but not as macho as an aluminium beer keg,
and ecologically more sound
than plastic webbing and plastic wrap.

An empty receptacle, the second-hand beercrate drifts,
becoming a platform for a speaker to stand on and address a crowd,
an extra seat at a party,
a shelf supporting a vase of flowers;
then forlorn, ending up as scrap,
splintered to firewood,
fed to flames.

Barnes Dance, Queen Street, Auckland

Crossing at the crossing on Cross Now,
where crossroads criss-cross, you cross
over crossing still, but lost to view
in crowds crossing now; crowd joins to
crowd in collective crossing, weaving
madly addled webs of rhythmic steps;
crossing and re-crossing rapidly reversed;
finding a personal way of moving, we
heel and toe it as it might be; trek to trot,
each foot as bulbs and root lifted up;
suits are jumping out of lifts to cross;
tripping, stamping, limping, we cross
back with the flow; lean and slide we go;
on the verge of twisting to turn we rise
to airy and delicate; make shifts of weight;
then dance inside our tubes of clothes;
do movement slivers, improv formations;
so break on through to pounce on up
past bus, car, truck; unweaving gladly,
heads shaken like pebbles from shoes –
till we've moonwalked to some place other;
jinked ankle bells in temples pedestrian;
and wended ways with dervishes whirling.

Elvis and the Vulcans

Midnight's gate sings the hosannas of Osama.
Vulcans stuck in quicksands, tied to the axle of Elvis,
praise depleted uranium like it's manna from heaven.
An Elvis-shaped grease-stain wavers over Texas.
Loose nukes sink the trigger-happy righteous,
who might wake, bloated in a blood tub,
soaking with tyrants, awash with petrodollars.

People want undead idols of trash tabloids:
popes, queens, madonnas, princes, and Elvis.
Elvis impersonators live in a town called Elvis.
Homeless push shop-trolley homes, sandbagged
with carrier bags packed with plastic collectables.
Aircraft carriers, stacked with choppers, sail
for the Retreat of Reason, as flags snap, drums flail.

Vulcans stub cigars out on corporate foreheads;
empty suits are cut to ribbons to open Gitmo.
Holy Joes close down hot lines, freeing masterminds
to roam across Uberstate as Vulcans. And signs
of Elvis hang from their talons, amidst weird,
sow-eared guinea pigs, dog-tagged malformations
of unknown known and known unknown situations.

Oh, these genetically-impaired raptor legends,
saluting flappily youth-oriented coffin fly-bys.
Hatched from an entropic planet's cracked skull:
a fatal, toxic, narcotic, alpha, human cargo
of plasticised, sanitised, collaterally-damaged,
striding, hooting, gliding, scurrying all sorts;
peons, serfs, minimum wage slaves, one-legged,
one-armed, monocular, missing bits and pieces,
headed to eternity, but proud of their country –
all leatherneck soldiers, on parade with Elvis.

Varieties of Religious Experience

Amidst crowd hiss from the deflated globe,
enter world eaters, led by a psychic robed.

Beards of prophets shaved, binned and biffed;
a wasted Christ between skyscrapers crucified.

Where deserts grow only missile silos,
sandstorm devils test the fatigue of faces.

Ghettoised gods go out on the ebb tide,
as colonised hulks under rust subside.

Saint Frappuccino, New Renaissance Man,
takes book club tours round the Holy Land.

Jog-trot militias surround camera crews
in muscle-flexed postures of twisted irony.

Dominos fall and raise panic of nations;
microphones launch funeral orations.

Thunderstorms of land mines dig mass graves,
while Google tells Google that Google saves.

All Armageddon replicas are logged;
all ends by disaster movies are clogged,

Empty thought balloons float over dunes:
Zen daydreams of a zillion hopeful sperm.

Some new planet finds the solar plexus centre,
its ocean arcs traced by an astronaut's finger.

Not Fit For Human Consumption

Molten metal smoke from cooking
computer-circuit boards is drifting
into a nostril's golden arch;
the climb to Paradise is vexed
by carbon trails of footprints.

The Amazon has a Brazilian wax;
Atlanta fishes out a suntan oil slick.
Gastropubs extrude from containers.
Jellyfish plastic bag shoals float
in surplus of redundant abundance.

Protesting at a five-star hotel, a goat
eats a cardboard Kentucky colonel.
Foodies scenery-munch Antarctic ice-caps.
Barbed-wire cross-hairs, trained on aviaries,
seek accompaniments for whale savouries.

Supermarkets sell not so much
frozen fish fingers, but fish arms,
fish stumps, as if answering to a need
for what doesn't exist, quick as a wink.
Slow boats barbecue on burnt-out oceans;
bleached-out rainbows leap can canyons.
Hurtling globalisation's highway, an oil rig
gets a blow-out, and flares like a sunspot.

Burn Rate

Their faces blob
and run in rain:
electric rain that sizzles,
burns to a stain.
They are thin
as phantoms,
and made of pixels.

A poetry book, whose greasy
pages flutter – like wallpaper
on a condemned building,
like ghosts gathering in a flurry –
begins to scorch and smoulder.

At night, dots climb from an oil well,
become dirt moving,
people moving,
a genome sequence moving,
points that glow like circles of hell.

What is the burn rate
of a quantum of atoms
that mushroom in explosion?

What is the burn rate
of galaxies that wheel
gaseous on a pin?

What is the burn rate
of sweat that showers
from the vaporous brows
of God?

Red Meat Roar

Turn critical mass back to year zero;
enter your brand; the product is: yes, you.
Love seeps through cells, staking a claim.
Midway to locking, though, where all dots
should come together, nothing quite fits –
take your skeletal state, your fur, your teeth,
said and done, just a mass of writhing insects,
we call this: before the time of the brand.

You can shop until the bomb, only your
name isn't here, so throw your challenge
down at an opening-up sale, where money
begs to serve, then be traced to vanish point:
cash nexus in blood plasma screened by heat.
You might get to live in rarefied air;
travel in a bubble, surrounded by stalkers –
brands need suspicions, feel bereft without.

Counter-intuitive, nevertheless accurate,
speak to missing persons after the tone;
find your new ground zero; enter the fray;
stab a finger till it shoots from the register.
If south-east district is not in service,
flee the perimeter Business Class to China;
do battle with the burka; swarm up like rain;
attract opposites to where they contradict.

Jack up a false ending, term it exit strategy,
as toxic waste chews your ear off and,
heard in the shadows, it's all strangled speech;
the praiseworthy found on treadmills of binge,

salvation disappearing before you arrive:
pockets pulled out, gestures throwaway,
displaced, replaced, armed with nothing,
yet breath, puffs of condensation, truly buoyant.

Song of the Market Actor

Can we pick up the numbers,
overhaul all front runners,

skip on by the velvet rope,
memorise the right manner,

fool any iris scanner,
grease a tell-tale itchy palm,

unearth sacred ancestors,
rip out the featherbedding,

be ground beneath a guru,
help to ease those growing pains,

trip the wires of persuaders,
reveal mounting inner fire,

behold our franchise options,
slip away the silken bonds,

learn how to last a lifetime,
appear in the final frame,

stay in touch, venture, get more,
push to ultimate levels,

then with a single gesture
blow in to chase down windfall,

roseate through sequinned night,
unforgiving at steel dawn?

Yes, till I take on too much,
toxic loss, your missing funds,
so that then come colder rains
screwing over hoped-for golden years —
in the crash of collateral damage,
love me, love my emotional baggage.

Kate Winslet Promotes a Credit Card

She's contorted over script or contract.

She mimes reading with hunched back.

She's somewhere inside *The New Yorker*.

She poses beneath the legend: *My life, my card.*

She sucks, like a straw or claw, at her finger.

She exposes, like that of a great ape, a foot's sole,

wrinkled as a map of the moon.

She has a big toe that seems so much older

than the rest of her, as if she has just

arisen from a bath, and that big toe

was under longest.

She has that toe as the punctum,

so that we must contemplate smoothness

wrinkled in a bath: that wrinkled, sensitive

point of balance exposed; just out of its shoe

and already cooling the blood.

In a photograph the colour of greyish tin,

she feels through the sole's drumskin

each reverberant step of her life.

She's architecture; she's an archive;

she's a firebird; she's a poet's metre,

putting her best foot forward.

Band Rehearsal

String player Ching hits the note too soon;
blames those poolside umbrella drinks he had with June;
so impatient Avalon bangs his big drum, boom;
a flambeau or two from Sammy M, the piccolo loon.
At a question flung from prickly Joe behind his bassoon,
which lingers like taste of bitter candy in a greasy spoon,
a crazy stillness enters the rehearsal gloom,
as if with the apparatus of a turf war it's been strewn;
but only with the hard cases of musicians is it festooned:
the grubstake of wild jazz is out of tune,
and nobody wants to talk about any elephant in the room.
The barflys' muse, she's from Rangoon;
leans against the doorframe in a fugue swoon;
wears a Shantung silk frock, coloured maroon;
begins to wooze through a bar-room croon,
pinching star-dust into a glass balloon.
Jittery as an amazon in a tailspin zoom,
she sings a beauty parlour blues, crying for the moon.

Beer Cans

There by cliff-top car-park we raise our beer cans'
                         warm foamy ziggurat
to the slowly buckling green Pacific carpet,
                        which sparkles its saltpans,
while birds flutter across the blue-eyed day
                        like eyelash mascara,
and sunlight bounces on afternoon's trampoline,
                        so joyously at play,
as marbled waves shoulder a rider in gleam
                        of black wet-suit to shore.

Poked fingers point balance over a parabola,
                        fathoming ocean curves,
before that crouched and slewed surfer, alive with nerves
                        atop booming breaker,
on crest of lustrous liquid steps, to cartwheel,
                        a da Vinci man stretched,
down through sudsy washing machine vortex,
                        like a boat's ploughing keel,
then from crumpled page of the storybook sea climbs
                        to paddle out once more.

Spent Tube

A cigarette after a long absence is like
revisiting haunts of my lost youth,
where I made a hollow claim or two in my time,
as the whole world danced to the same smoky tune
before we all swore off that infernal bridegroom,
that fictive fig-leaf curling up into the cut-
and-dried statement of ciggy threads set alight
and blazing at once like Balzac on caffeine,
us party-goers of manic erudition,
juggling wee small hours the other side of midnight,
where bees are smoked from bonnets
at the behest of rollies dancing in the hands of the voluble,
toccatas of talkativeness until night becomes day,
with gesticulated odes to *Drum* or 'Winnie Reds'
beneath some tobacco god's revered smoked head,
tribute of such fiery tabernacles of tobacco
as to be a rakehell's cat-scratch fever sated,
yet still in love with its poisonous fumes,
its wavering mirages stitched from skeins
of wraiths wreathed into bleakly elegant pose,
its ash that deft fingers conjure dreams from,
in medicine man or peace pipe ceremonies,
glow of satisfaction below the level of language,
at smoko,
by the side of the road,
by a doorway, by a swill-bucket,
with a man who jokes,
trapped in rings of chain-smoke,
expelling voluminous puffs
much as if he's smoking himself,
tarry vapour sucked down off-kilter,

to calm jumpy nerves,
until it falls like a dud from nerveless fingers,
or from the lips of dying warriors,
the last heroic puff in a newsreel,
spent tube but still dancing spot of light,
because the cigarette I was smoking then
has not yet been stubbed out.

The Zero

With a writhe of hands,
this world-famous nobody,
a vacuum really,
an elbow plucker, one of the fans,
casting about for a way to be felt,
makes a once-in-a-lifetime offer
to become frontrunner;
and this unedited emotional genius,
flirtatious pathological liar,
name-dropper, debt-dodger,
silent taunter, foe,
personal confessor,
wreck on the never-never,
Olympian, winner, game-on
whooper punching air,
this hero ready to go –
is then gone.

Traffic Checkpoint

Such intoxication, moments before
the breathalyser, then the fissure that
opens up along the dotted line – it's
something to burrow into. We might
debate the question of salvation, while
behold a moon astronaut – eyes revealed
in the rear-vision mirror – who answers
a few questions through the air-lock window.
Eyes chase the wandering light that shines
from a torch in befuddled wonder – so
might chance remarks let the random enter.
Let's see, can I remember the gesture,
and does the gesture remember me? No
sweet tune's picked out on the fretboard,
since the song sucks, like vinyl cracked
and worn. The engine grinds, corrosive
as a night split by klaxons, the throbbing
cop shop's sour miasma of busted drunks.

Christchurch Gothic

Summer's Avon spelt the names of atua in green,
and through trees sun shafts dug at dappled lawns,
as if to unearth a circuit-board of worm-holes,
the universe beneath the labyrinth,
the silent presence of mountain shingle
across the curve of the island's waist.

Teen racers hummed like bees in a hive,
and late autumn was the harlequin
hurrying past them down Bealey Ave,
towards the rusted, busted, midnight hour,
its sword-and-sorcery pageant of flashing sabres,
its chorus lines of black on moonlit runnelled iron.

They drained the swamp for bodies,
and found a city in a smog overcoat the colour
of mid-winter: a swallowed-up netherland.
Around it, paddock windbreaks rose in ranks,
long shadows falling like guillotines,
as night exhaled its nausea.

Frosted spring melted into this deep carpet,
and from Port Hills rolled the squared-away harvest,
whose matted roots expressed pedigrees of settlement,
a holding pattern of heartbeats, brainwaves, fingerprints
down blind alleys. The city breathed in –
a hot air balloon sailed above its festoons of bitumen.

Night Patrol in a Psychic Shellhole

*(a reflex response to James Robinson's Light Touch mixed media
exhibition at the Mark Hutchins Gallery, Wellington, March 2009)*

Starters red as tamarillo or raw venison,
accompanied by the pink babble of tongues
in Wanaka or Henderson;
a smell of petrol, flash of kebab scimitars,
café echo of steel strings
from just-played guitars, sonics of solar wind,
cigarillo whiffs puffed from wound-down windows
of Cuba Street's vintage cars,
making as if inside his cranium
it's snowing on Mars.

Don't get him started on his chainsaw manifesto,
where he's making a clearing in the bush,
channelling John and Yoko,
while watching amphibians leap for the trees.
Got lift-off like a rocket from a silo,
and his meat-rack skeleton dangles in the breeze,
and his press-ganged television is a black hole rush,
out of which poison rain for the soul bleeds,
decayed to an utter-grey crush
of germy ooze a-go-go.

Gets inside your blind spot, and starts to meet your eye;
seizes on microdramas, and blows them sky-high.
Peek in at his windows,
as if disdainful of disease beneath undone flies –
but somewhere between stigma, stigmata,
smegma, and stick it mate,
he makes you see niceties can turn out to be lies.
The shrunken heads of modern-day psychologies
decorate his mantelpiece singing a cantata –
listen to their tiny cries.

Stark as a million-man-march to tootle and drum, ants
track where he paints on trench coat, cast-off pants,
or tarp salvaged from a hangi pit,
merry as a muppet beneath façade of filth,
with cauliflower ears and virile nose hairs,
the twisted vista of a big face that rants
bag-lady style, with the beauty of the health-
damaged, best seen in unnatural light,
yet sad-eyed in all-too-human defiance –
a revealed creature of fragile happenstance.

He sews in white, tooth and nail, and as spiders can,
he cobwebs the trap shut, gets under your skin,
to summon child armies of redemption,
then builds a butterfly net of red thread
to capture abandonment's tremulous dread,
until breaking news is finally broken
against the needle-click of emptiness.
He whistles like a tohunga to wake the dead,
but when the airbrush has spoken,
it is the alien, the other, he has woken.

Out of scorched earth purple spurts,
like smears of bougainvillea blossom,
or streaks of monster blob putty ectoplasm,
or brightest bogan camouflage uniform
in which a kid slouches, boom shudder boom,
to ignite the room – a shellshocked soldier
whose wounds have been cleansed by maggots,
or a Coast-to-Coaster
with fathomless levels of ticker,
chasing the flow down through the river.

Belief in the Pacific

Yes, night's nowhere, that's where I sleep;
till the sun wakes, stretches, begins to burn,
and greets me when my eyelids, dazzled, leap.

Sunday's hymns laze on ocean's horizon.

Cloud feathers sand white, as green seethes
across taro leaves, across palm fronds' weave;
and coconut trees vault to the blue sky
clang of church bells.

            A man bows to consult
his Bible; thumbs verse like a hitchhiker,
smooth brow filled with lagoon's light,
though engine drone drowns surf's sigh.

From sleep's hurricane my mind heaves
its woven mats; and I'm this wind-drifter
with fraying map, dreaming of a comeback.

Suva Hibiscus

Dawn's green brooch,
unfurled brolly,
silver cocoon,
opened grubby
jar of lollies,
dusty colours
on festival floats.
Orange tubas,
pink gliders,
purple flags,
torn petal rags
in free fall,
saluted by ants,
the cockroach.
Frail satellite
dish, tracking noon
and ocean charts.
Blossom ear-hung,
ukelele strum,
scarlet signature,
rain's nodding drum.
Shrivelled ember,
or white as snow,
we bare our hearts
to your glow.

Between Viti Levu and Tongatapu

Angel wings froth beneath the propellor
as salt foam that surface hysterics mirror.

Edges of cyclones caress
family ancestors in their graves,
and plough beaches like a resurrection.

Time's ascension swims up in shrouds
of bubbles from caverns where seeds grew
years ago, having ripened on mango trees.

Coral grit taps the glass of flash hotels,
their lawns shaded by razor fronds.

Sunset's ripened mango colours rot to
thunderheads, dark as rum's demons wrung from
an undertow of clouds soaked by the sea.

Some sharks circle the hull,
white comets diving through green swelling
gardens of suddenly flowering rain.

Nuku'alofa

Breeze bangs doors shut,
and a peppery drizzle
grinds out of the sea,
until with fluttery heartbeat
then steady pulse, emerges
a chorus of birthday girls
in their summer of youth,
their happiness of legs,
running through dry gutters,
down the freshening road,
over the hot trapped breath
of town, bringing cool
drenching laughter, glee,
rippling quick ribbons
to tickle across skin,
over plants quivering,
eager in the face of rain,
drops that splash on frogs,
shiny new coins lapped
in a wishing well there.

Drowned Volcano

The plane drones across mattress kapok
to follow the crease-marks of the atlas
over a blue haze where outer islands
rise amongst dolphins, humpback whales.
Islands there, pulsing with breadfruit sap,
unwrap tapa mats from coconut cordage.
The flukes and tails of those islands thwack,
then shimmer back beneath ocean spray.

Outer islands under trade-wind flags sail,
showered in storms of frangipani stars.
Untamed sea horses swim with them through
nights maned in swirls of dark rum;
and garlands of surf decorate them.
Days, lit up with guava fragrance, bud
into banyan roots, flowers of wild banana,
candlenut trees, sweet mango's sacrament.

Only now does the smudge of the Great Wall
of China café burning become visible.
Only now do rusty freighters and fleets
begin to leak as if they cannot stop,
and the jelly-green glass wobble with tadpoles
that strain to break into toads the size of trucks.
The sky drains its kava bowl, the sea chucks
up a tsunami of canned Pacificana,

and a jack-in-the-box is surfacing
amid shoals, reefs, sands, as a sign:
a drowned volcano risen on a raft
of birthstones loosened from the globe's grip.
A scorched cinder cone, it climbs and shines.
It might herald the re-entry of Christ
into the Pacific, or a radioactive atoll,
ringing an alarm for the end of time.

Steve Irwin Way

The Glasshouse Mountains float on the horizon.
Their strange shapes fill the morning.
They are rum casks rolled down from Bundaberg,
or old pagoda bells unearthed
from a ballasted world of giants.
Steve Irwin Way switches like a croc's tail,
and the shapes vanish as Noosa traffic roars.
Daylight is on slow burn, all grease vapour
and hot air, a sugar fix hitting home.
Reptile eyes surface from cappuccino swamps,
the hills wait to speak with fire's tongue.
Gums sift light and ooze hospital balms,
my sandals feel as slippery as mango skins.
Ironic caws of rooftop crows
sound out noon's scheme of things,
waves of stink ripple through the nose.
Leaves are gnawed into brocade by insects,
bark coffins sewn for their congregations.
High rollers run the sun's lucent comb
over surf shrivelling to freckled foam.
Surfers rise to cumulus peaks and pours
above ghostly jellyfish men-o'-war,
as if to join the white-bellied eagle's soar,
then tumble like pigeons towards an ecstasy,
a rush of bubbles, the laughing buddha of the sea.

Win Seven Days in Sydney

As each day might breeze past the felt steam
of our slow breathing, with dawn risen orange
from black lacquerwork of eucalyptus groves;
mango syrups that dry inside bins by curbs;
joggers sweat-gilded; dog-walkers also glossed;
hum of a storm approaching on blue horizons
of the superstructure; rimes of brine that climb
beaches; smog the mauve of violin music; chrome
that taps shiny claves to set azure ablaze; waves
of windscreens a din of beaten gold at Bondi.

Buff, pink, tan, cream pegged between bikinis.
Heat fires light left to shovel its own pizza oven.
The sun smells of tar, brimstone, shiraz, ozone.
Tablecloth ties are worn to lunch, but no one's there.
Noon rakes every face with a crystal gaze. We've
been here seven days, tasting the glare lacing up
shadows in queued-for sorbets of lemon and lime.
So this is the summer of the seventeenth year.
The Opera House yawns and bares glitter-fangs;
blossoms buckle; ants raise nail-parings in thanks.

Evening's kettle lets it settle to boil again.
Streamers break-dance like tea-leaf confetti,
up swirling over trees and sinking through them.
Fruitbats wrap themselves in darkest Darlinghurst.
Lattice knits up lattice to web the fiery nest.
Poltergeists fling thunderous furniture skywards,
as bare feet patter on lightning's floorboards,
and pin numbers spin roulette wheels of jailed saints,
raining sweat for God, who doesn't appear, though
big spaces compress to nothing between airports.

Lines at Wharf's End

Summer's evening gown ruffles gold silk;
saxophones of stars tilt;
surf ebbs, and beach guitars plink;
conch shells of cloud squeal to pink;

breezes trumpet the sun's farewell;
a flagging cabbage tree rustles its leaves;
night throbs on rusty reefs of roofs;
marimbas of town lights melt towards overseas.

A Nation's State

The whinger, the skite, the wowser,
the left-out, the shunted-off, the tumble-dried,
two-fisted tub-thumpers, lunatic moon lovers,
swoony-voiced heapers-up of praise,
doomsters, gloomsters, all-time losers,
the numberless numb

the comrade, the sister, the brother,
the parents, the bastard offspring,
the doers and the hooers, the munted,
those living on a prayer,
those holding up the world with their shoulders,
carriers of bloodied Xmas cards

product demonstrators, supermarket couponistas,
wicket-takers, wicket-keepers, applauders,
stakeholders waiting to be stroked,
backslappers, storm-chasers, clothes horses,
spirit mediums, falsifiers, straight arrows,
characters made of newsprint, celebrities made of pixels

fake editors, junior pleasers, also-rans,
the shopped-in, the convictionless, the blind-sided,
told-you-so's, sweatshop owners, boatshoe people,
backroom boffins, knowledge wallahs, keepers of keys,
the bare-knuckled, the trans-oceanic, the touch-sensitive,
the undead forever

glorybox embezzlers, sticklers for etiquette,
ear-benders anon, talkback's hanging judges,
chin-up daylight savers, night-robber brethren,
mutton kings riding in ambulances,
movie bee wranglers with a zillion bees to house,
phone flash-mobs demobilising one by one by one

How to Big Yourself Up

Be the bloviating blogger who blogs on, dusk till red dawn;
be the sixth billionth sand grain to encroach on beachfront lawn;
be the crazy whitefella razzin on the didgeridoo;
be geek-orthodox totty in phat pants, goin the whole hog
    barbecue;
be a pre-teen human-gene kung fu kangaroo;
be marijuana mujahadeen dancing to Arabian drums;
be the only happy-clappy one stopping to twiddle your thumbs;
be a coalition of contradictions helping out populations with
    their financial complications;
be a turntablist spinning full-bore in a sweat-lodge tepee;
be a blitz chess champion obsessed by slow-moving reality tv;
be the lonesome spoiler shouting from a rooftop rendezvous for
    secret lovers;
be a pop-eyed phobic loon placing ransom notes between
    bestseller covers;
be an über-baby-boomer wearing poppety socks which tick-tock
    with sky-blue clocks;
be a Butoh mime brewing rivers of yak-butter tea that trickle
    down the Everest of humanity;
be a soul sister disco diva disciplining disciples with visions of
    the Ecstasy Tablets of Saint Teresa;
be the line dancer who does a soft shoe shuffle at the CAT scan,
    leaping from hospice wheelchair;
be there when a bimbo eruption erupts because Bollywood's
    come to town, offering all of us a part;
be a Portuguese man o' war made of salty tears, but still shooting
    for the moon from desolate deserts of the heart;
do not mean but be forever: big yourself up.

Bards of Paekakariki

(for Michael O'Leary)

Behold Paekakariki where late sun trawls,
throwing nets of light across strong seas
to the afternoon anchorstone of Kapiti.

Surf sighs out its test-match cheers
that echo on from yesteryear,
like the engine rush of departing trains,
or dance-band songs in the local hall.

Froth subsides with a shush on shingle;
then from dense bush a swaggie roves.
He, out of swamp forests of the brain,
trudging up along the sand, strives
to knot with twine his coat of green.

From his swag tumble bays and coves;
sheep like brooches from pockets fall.
Scarves of scrub he pegs on hillsides;
he gathers armfuls of flowering lilies;
glides slopes plunged giddy to the flat,
as sunset flees from pink rambler roses
swathed in the dust of roadside verges.

Days are an indigestible richness,
that sneak off and leave us in the dark,
just now as clifftops drop away.
Days end in boil-ups of puha and mutton flaps,
in storms hurling land back to stone and bone.
Dwellers here choose a poem without words,
discovering words tremble over truths.
They scrape fat from their plates in silence,
content at last with the marrow of existence.

Dada Dunedin

For I will consider Dunedin, for you are a brackish backwater
     inhabited by south sea gods.
For, tipped out of a colonial toy-box, your stone buildings
     mingle with the bones of the land.
For oystercatchers by night, above Knox Church, cluck and
     chuckle, flying seawards.
For you have villas, with diamonded mullions blazing, and
     glossy cast-iron lace-work whose doily fringes hang above
     verandas.
For you have villas decaying and tomb-like, mantelpieces
     crammed with empty bottles and medication.
For Robbie Burns in bronze plucks a quill from a passing gull,
     and writes on air words in praise of Octagon hip-hop.
For at your centre you have a shiny Gaggia espresso machine.
For within your castle keep are the witch hats and wizard cones
     of pinnacles and turrets, cloak draperies, and a vault
     possessing the Harry Potteresque desk of the Ettrick
     Shepherd James Hogg.
For your bees nuzzle summer's clouds, and your skateboarders
     scrape out pavement's song, and shadows drawn from trees
     run across your parks in the late afternoon.
For Jetty Street on Sunday is loud with the eerily magnified
     musical whispers of industrial rust, and guitar fuzz buzzing
     like sourly ground-up sawdust.
For Anzac poppies bloom in Picardy Street, and orange cordials
     are poured on Alhambra's sports fields.
For every other corner on Princes Street echoes to bagpipe
     skirls, horse hooves clatter, and phantom flow of golden
     syrup ragtime piano solos.
For Rattray Street remembers the boogie-woogie, the elective
     jazz mutes, the wah-wah pedallers and the doesy-does
     beneath zigzag steps.

For King Edward Street is greasy with the taste of Southern Fried Gothic, and loud with rugby choruses from beer-babblers at the Brook.

For your seagulls glide up and down George Street looking to greet all they happen to meet.

For your mollusc-like dwellings are concealed by tough thorny hedges.

For you have your pipe-dreams of a harbour bridge and railway tracks elevated above a statue of Queen Victoria surfing.

For you still possess the ruined grandeur of some cavernous Edwardian gin palace populated by elderly alcoholics.

For you are a synonym for depopulation, petrified as limestone, with your buried tunnels leading to bricked-up bomb shelters and closed gold smelters.

For you are a clue to all of New Zealand, a primal bog of settlement which has evolved to spawn many of the nation's symbols of self-identification.

For who knew what could grow inside your cocoon of will and idea.

For there are rumours of beetles munching their way through your museum, over the notched spears and sandstone sinkers, the basalt adzes and bones of birds.

For you are a jester in cap and bells holding up an inflated gallbladder on a stick, which vibrates in the wind like an aerial tuned to otherworldly hymns.

For in the New Year you are a ghost ship of a town maintained by a tatterdemalion skeleton crew in op-shop regalia.

For the sight of you spread out in the skylarking sun reveals postal districts packed with concealed email users.

For you stretch up, Dunedin, take a breath, and sunk in dreamtime vacancy seek to break the trance of a hundred years, aware in your cobwebbed obstinacy that you're making an exhibition of yourself again.

New Chants of Ngati Katoa

A microphone
prods forest silence.

Bandwagons vent spleen
on late night radio's phone-in.

Cutting up rough at a reunion,
the boys give it guts;
they give it guts;
they park their trucks;
and they give it heaps of guts.

Dancing woo-hooey masters of world
economics con the national mood,
preaching hoo-ha of the sinking lid.

Editors of infotainment in their wisdom
deliver a sermon
on hierarchies of the rubbish tip.

Fifteen Wallabies,
bombed by a bucket
of weedkiller,
are rendered zombies
on Eden Park's turf.

Gallipoli sand grains
chase through an hourglass
to surpass
heights of mountains.

Hallowed salutations get squeezed to chur,
whazzup and bro, by Muzza and Gazza
raising a stinkfinger.

Ingarangi marches to the pub for his daily noggin,
with bagful of shag and pocketful of scroggin.

Jake the Muss jollies Jase the Face,
to throw handfuls of hot quarrel
on an architectural-
award-winning raised roof.

Kiwi is a shy pet given to bush walks,
sticky-beaking, squawks,
and long distance travel by jet.

Last bastion of the fat lamb farmer
becomes butter-lust of the dairy farmer.

Mother of the nation, Hine-Nui-Te-Po,
is tohunga transgender with a Celtic moko.

Novelisations of local situations
gaze at navel after navel
within quiet rim after quiet rim
of volcano after volcano.

Open slather of the coast's green curving cone,
poured with kauri gum, mountainous ice-cream,
and behold: hokey-pokey's triple star reborn.

Parliamentary piss-artists take the cake:
flown with wine,
they toast vintage gossip straight from the vine.

Quizzical James McKenzie,
locked up in Lyttelton,
peering from the shroud of an oilskin,
is used to sell the high country.

Red-stained salads and sour aromas
rise from Beetroot Belters: vinegar
wit let out grudgingly through false choppers.

Stuffed armchair
critics elect to wallpaper
the view over.

Time to heat electric jugs and fill thermos flasks;
time to pull on wool socks;
time to raise backpacks;
time to stow hacky sacks,
time to put aside daily humdrum tasks.

Using inspired guesswork to gain refugee status,
the Devil is a postulant from some other country.

Vern Acular, that good keen bloke,
is the new big hopes
pastoral manager talking a blue streak up the boohai,
and he's got my vote, yes sirree Bob, he's got my vote.

Waist-deep in wool-pile carpets of embassies,
tongue stuck out: the tiki's a dollar sign in a waste of signs.

Xmas is our backside of the year,
when rose moles and tattoos we bare
all in stipple to the sun's pied beauty.

Your doolally walk
is a parody of Ponsonby beefcake,
as on the wild side you mince
through Rotorua's Hell's Gate.

Zealots with zeal are doing a haka:
kia kaha kia kaha,
hold fast, be strong, be strong:
the chant of us all, the Ngati Katoa
stompalong, stompalong.

Jailbird at Momona Airport

He kārearea ahau ...

I come from the bay of hawks.
Propellers roar my tragedy.
I roar my own ecstasy.
I'm exiled where I walk.
I drool. I hang on my own talk.
I'm between jails coiled in a shroud.
Enter shackled at wrist and ankle.
My feet are bare. I rankle.
I'm off to where I'm sent.
But my stare is proud.
The howl of the mongrel.
The fool's toothless scowl.
My tinny shack paid back.
Tinfoil, flame and the glass bowl.
I drank. I trespassed. Now I rage.
I don't utter sounds of doubt.
My rhetoric is renegade.
I return to thoughts of dak.
I chew my cheek. I'm made.
My toes claw the floor.
I am silent as a waiting gun.
I stare at the sun.

Soundings

Caught in the ear of the wind,
silence stretches for an instant,
then to summer's racket succumbs:
children shrilling out a need;
a doorbell by hawkers thumbed;
pavements alive with clicking heels;
the cool white noise of news, urgent
to natter and bleed through walls.

Growl of bus, beep of car horn,
construction sites to eavesdrop on;
generations making dissent and din –
whine, groan, roar, moan, hum.
Sounds spelling it out as song:
shivery nuances, rising pitches,
acoustic ripples, transmission glitches,
snap of teeth and bubblegum pop.

The uphill grunt, the glottal stop,
the hit tune warbled from the shower,
while furtherest stars since their birth
have been singing like a lawnmower
on a fine Saturday afternoon,
heard from so far away from earth
it's almost not heard, no more than
absent hiss on a sonic detector.

Yet we cheer them to their very echo:
sing you singers – the time of singing
is not over yet, so sing, echo on echo.
Sounds of many call over the bay;
carry me back, they sing to us;
and in the end all are chosen;
our songs lifted from below,
torn from earth to float away.

Oh that voice of God technique,
those chords of glory, that grandiose talk,
those notes raised by an orator leaping:
Holy musicola, and do-rag promises,
old hee-haw of the donkey caravan;
or snicker-snacker-snick of barber scissors;
Nazi bellow at the Nuremberg Rally –
a cut-off, chicken-plucking horrid squawk.

For the dolphin language, they say,
has twelve thousand semi-tones;
and there's a magic drone that blesses
those who feel it – *have you heard, have you heard?*
I have heard monkish choirs, skeletons tap-dancing,
seventy-six trombones, a hurdy-gurdy that swirled,
blood's steady drumbeat, polychromatic cellphones:
all sounds speaking with the mouth of the world.

At Macraes Flat

See the round hill's lone tree planted for war dead,
who soldier on year after year, though gone;
yesterday's clammy fog blown free, tufts anchored
tentative, like lambswool snagged by dry thistle,
or suds from wash-tub rest-cures for work clothes.

Caught off-balance, a bumble-bee falls to dart
from the car whisking through butter-and-egg-yolk light
making golden rabbit pie crust, thyme's hare sauce;
windscreened rush past tussock pulse, lake bristle,
bleached peaks, stacked stone house roofless in sunshine.

Rubbled sheep exercise their right to be a flock.
Curved like clouds, hiding skinks, rocks emerge,
ribbed as if scarred by frost snap, hail scratch, wind grip.
Their sky-staring angles patched with flaking lichen,
silhouetted heads of petrified gods, they stud slopes;

and rise from craters dug deep, daffodils dust-caked,
pig pelts hung to cure on a farm fence by the hundred;
while haulers jolt schist, drag ore searched for by blade-tip;
till, the whole day shredded down to sea level and dark,
the car follows the road along a cracked-open spark.

Kōauau

Oracles of mist reach
to sea-foam volumes
a feather touch
at the river's mouth,
breakers the only pressure
solitude feels
as evening's fronds
mark golden glare
on the brows of ranges,
moon's risen skull
grinning at a West Coast
so brooding and so dark
it might be made of coal.

Aotearoa Considered as a Scale Model

(for Hone Tuwhare, 1922–2008)

South's a museum where the muses live,
en masse, corralled in glacial beauty,
their upper slopes hunched shawls of white,
their bridal veil falls a drowning roar –
eroded real estate that scrubs up fine.
Glazed-over lakes have their memories;
tow-ropes of cloud fray on mountain ranges.
Winds enfold and tuck in towns like kids;
shelvings of hail button up roads;
snow shadows daylight to the marrow.

Up North, Hei Tiki wreathes a green tongue,
flicker-tastes darting lizards of rain.
For the New Zealand land mass rain's opium,
deliquescent as it stills and calms.
Earth trembles under a lone waterdrop
from a cloud bank you knock and enter,
threaded with wet to sew the mist shut.

Hot underbellies grow entities of wool;
outlandish floods chase down crowns of fire.
Buckled, rubbled, gullied, thorny and flexed,
ragamuffin farms dig their hooks into you.
The paddock next door's the place buses go
to sink on their springs, lose bits and rust;
rising about them gently grows long grass.

If shabby corduroy paddocks won't wash,
follow a jiggle-string of beach pulled taut
by the soaraway kite of blue sky,
as Tangaroa unfolds a pill-flecked jersey.
Glory then in creation, its nature
a miracle where you add all this water
to quake's uplift, gigantic in aspect,
at zero hour the indissoluble ego.

Landscape for Breakfast

Moths in brocade wing it to darkness;
dawn flames from tabernacles of stars;
gold crosses of grass glimmer, meshed by frost.
Shadows trickle down crevices sheep cross;
the breeze that blows gnaws the sweet sap.

Bulls sacrificed on freezing works' hooks skid
to oblivion, and day's melody trembles
amid bellow, bleat, and risen hawk's cry.
The Hawkduns' dry tussock fluffs with snow;
years come on like a far-off avalanche.

Above glints of fencewire and cobweb strands,
the sky is a wide-trayed ute, loaded down
with wool skerricks, lambs' tails, fleeces piled shorn,
headed on through the back-country coastwards.

Sun's pulse on gecko-jewelled stone knuckles –
a geology sculpted into fists,
waters weave and unweave down gorges –
the poem of land brings itself forth:
englobed in shine like pounamu,
and ranged across the breadth of Otago;
with taste of roadside dust and hay stalks crushed,
with buildings that scrabble, dig for purchase,
with windmill vanes that sing power-line songs,
as the wind draws back coverlets of leaves,
and troughs pressure eye-knots of weather.

The sea blossoms green salt from fathoms,
its heaving forest enclosing a storm
to roar to hot earth's core, and dine on foam.

The Harbour

Rainbow's edge soaks up time,
December opens its album,
we welcome days with flowers,
form clouds to thread high tides,
silver touches our fingertips,
freshest almonds press their oils,
and cordite is a valve for fire.

Eyes sewn tight with teardrops,
violet penumbras under lashes,
the point of her tongue a bustle
of fizzy atoms, blood oranges,
rare earths, trace minerals,
pepper, clove, cinnamon, her
skin smelling of petrol and tin,
we hear the radio play house,
house keeps it under its hat.

How to harbour a harbour's Sunday,
its woolly Zeppelin self aloft?
Bees, a team in striped sports kit,
unbundle their goal-questing as
an embrace of wings around apple
blossom crowding the panes that open
on harbour's steely water, darkened
to the shade of the windscreen of the
red car towing a speedway wreck
by trailer along Portobello Road.

Brewer's mash, coal smoke, sugar drift,
a late burst of cadmium lemon light
when afternoon greases up to evening,
and the harbour's turquoise cathedral
shimmers, as if covered with fish scales,
or frocked in satin of Virgin Mary blue,
before turning amethyst as evening's sky,
then ebbing, weed-woven, stinky, stapled
in by rusted ironmongery and bitumen,
crumbled clods risen to an old church
with sharp steep pitch, above which
muscular hills flex before falling away
to crumpling surf, white sheets on a bed,
ocean breathing out brushings of wild silk.

Summer Hail

Summer is searching for shady verandas,
fingertips moving over shrubs and crockery.
Each window fine-tunes a crystal angle,
venetians run cool stripes over greenery,
as time is knocked into the hat held out
by clowning child or grown clown's memory.

The dog is ropeable, he barks and barks,
at bulging garden hose, mad as the cut snake
that mimics a traffic-directing cop in motion,
or thrash of someone stood on the garden rake;
while our hands grab at handles, pluck weeds,
wring out togs, and wave for old time's sake.

Those black-and-white photos with yellow tint,
you have to dig down to where they're buried:
they show us kids going on an expedition;
playing backyard cricket looking worried;
or laughing squint-eyed against the sun's glint;
always holding out whatever find we carried.

A kitchen sieve clangs as if about to sift
heaped flour for sponge cakes of nostalgia.
Light heel-tap of spoon, roar of the mixer;
and the iron roof rattling kettle drums
above rooms which darken when hail comes –
the rooms where shades of summer drift.

Winter, She Said

The tumble-drum drier churns
clothes you left when you left.
Tree frogs into dark waters leap;
skinks through bouldered crevices slide;
a dulcimer is strummed in the casbah.
Puff-cheeked clouds chase sunset's shadows
across quilted fields of Canterbury.
Wasps have built a paper nest.
Gloom surrounds the fading house,
and its chamber music of doleful door hinges.
Chopping wood in winter as wasps hum –
from summer's zenith it's a long way down.
Kindling unlatches
at the catch of flame –
stacked wood roars like an angry man.
Sawn-up coffins of nameless insects
melt to a red glow.
Night switches on darkness
room by room;
recess rises from recess;
windowpanes glisten.
An anorexic moon
slips from a smother
of ferns, a cradle of branches,
and glides with a glimmer
towards a pincushion of stars,
leaving nothing but the touch of moths and frost.

Cricketers of the Eighties

In primary school I buckled pads on
to learn cricket's formal grammar,
how it built hours of prose, moments of poetry,
from architecture of six sticks, two small planks,
and the crack and smack of shot from pitch.

In the classic stroke, bat collides with ball,
which is hurled to hang in the outfield;
airborne it looms, avoiding hands of welcome.
The ball touches down alone, then is flung
in vexation back to its keeper at the wicket.

Dug in at the crease, I flicked at spinners,
but didn't often thump the earnest half-volleys
other boys served up. We were like chess pieces:
in white, on a green board teachers controlled.
Summer found us in long grass looking for the ball.

Forward to the Eighties, watching New Zealand's
eleven – legendary as Ian Botham's gut,
or broadswordsmen, or poets with Curnow's
wild iron – whacking Oz then England in Tests,
to make sinewy syntax articulate.

There was Hadlee, a scorching nor'wester
sailing from a clear sky, gusting at batsmen;
from his arms' bent longbow a red arrow
launched at the stumps, fielders arrayed like posts
of a pa palisade, ready with haka leaps.

Hadlee on stride, a catapult on one leg,
back leg a rudder, lobbed the ball so it bobbed
off-kilter, but sprang beneath the bat to shave
off bails, before batsman, slanted at the slats,
had grasped that the wicket had been taken.

And batsman Martin Crowe, who could help
the ball, once or twice, soar like the Remarkables;
or swat it away to the height of a hill;
or clobber the sphere square-cut for four,
shake his waka paddle, then just lean, weight on bat.

Glenn Turner sometimes swung a haymaker;
other times, all day, he built a stone wall,
but snagged the ball to steal a run or two.
He could lock up batting with strategic play;
with sure motion make the game drift his way.

The Tall Man

(for Hardwicke Knight, 1911–2008)

The tall man stoops,
becomes the nonagenarian,
bending into a question-mark, a spiral,
child-like,
an embryo curled round time's injuries.
The great rock they crushed the ore from
has gone.
Into that box.
A long white cloud of hair is streaming,
tufting into wings,
into a twinkle-toed walker,
on a clean-swept floor,
in the stillness of the starry sky.
Are six enough to carry out
the funeral rites of the mind?
The iron tongue of some great bell
is tolling its doleful chant
to the hand-me-down city.
Wombed, then housed, then coffined,
daylight secretes its silences,
and expires like a flame.
Any life is a story to be told
in shadows thrown by a lamp:
under lunar light, a dark halo,
a trembling staccato of shadows.
After winter trees, spring
will bud to feel the gnarled future.

Where the Big Rivers Go

Rangitaiki, Waihou, Mohaka,
        Ngaruroro – Pacific-wards;
                Waikato, Whanganui, Rangitikei,
        Manawatu, Whangaehu, Mokau –
all into the Tasman.
        The Clutha, Taieri, the Clarence,
                Waitaki, Waiau, Waimakariri
        of Te Wai Pounamu – the Pacific;
and Wairau goes Cook Strait.

        Savage waters fall from hems of snow,
                tea-coloured, frothy, or flow clear.
                        Slower swans might crane their necks
                towards a floating hide, a sheep
        carcase submerged amongst beetles and flies;
then a dolphin on the breaking wave:
        big-finned surf runner's glide
                towards laughing gulls airborne,
        quivery as a tree in a gale.

                Raked by rain, the open mouth.
                        Bubbles rise to curtain in grey
                                the water serpent, elusive mako,
                        smoking wind and spume –
        mists that uncurl their wairua.

A school of yellow-eyed mullet,
        caught by wind-shear currents,
                plunges under smacks: trawler
                        dynamics wear schools down further
                through sonics. Raptures deep and high run

from ice-bridge brows of silent mountains,
their stone goblets, their waterfalls pure
dream of that motion of the sea
that makes boulders knock, shingle click,
and tumbles glass
the frosted amber of kauri.

Paua

On a beach covered in ashtrays,
the ocean the human faces
can raise the earth,
gnashed to render
fragments in an instant –
smashed paua shell
shot through with lustre,
gilded baloney of tat;
but what colour is that
exactly, groans the hell
of the hydrothermal vent
with expelled hiss of breath –
scrupulous and tender green,
or dust motes in a cave's beam?

Tārawhirimātea, God of Winds, Visits the Province of O

On this blowy evening in high summer,
all tassels of toetoe are dipped in aura,
and tarry roads are pulling Dunedin taut,
like stout ship's ropes,
as if the whole brick-and-stone shebang
was about to launch oceanwards
in search of some further shore,
with the sky
holding the moon's thin scythe,
for harvesting pumpkins,
watercress, clumps of borage,
wild blue flowers flickering.

Clouds, white as the paper bags
wearing the initial of McDonalds
blowing in the wind down George Street,
turn gold in dying rays,
like tattered battleflags of brigades,
whose remnants lodge in cemeteries
the length and breadth of the Province of O,
in a region given over to remembrance,
through war memorials and parkland statues,
of a lingering imperial past.

And, as a nor'wester rises through the asphalt
jungle of North East Valley
between houses ploughing down the green swell
and up the other side like flotillas of boats,
lifting on its buoyancy, on its updraught,
supermarket carrier bags full of wind,
full of the breath of Tārawhirimātea, god of hot air,
the gliders have descended at Omarama,
and open-tops of sports cars have closed at Oamaru,
for Tārawhirimātea has begun to gallop along the coast
like Four Horsemen of the Apocalypse,
like the Hounds of Heaven, like the Grim Reaper,
and with pentecostal force divine on whirlwind tour,
become the twister travelling through Kurow
that picks up a herd of kunekune pigs
to transport them shuddering down the road,
while cats cartwheel to use up all their lives,
and trees dance fandangos branch to branch.

Tārawhirimātea the dust-devil flings horseshoes,
scraps of rust, and howls outside doors of pubs,
and hurries off in all directions to arrive everywhere at
    once,
and with one last gesture dumps, like barrels of bowling
    club
champion rosettes, a ruddy sunset glow
over the ranges of the Province of O,
till the next thing, night turns off the light,
so the glow is stuffed and Tārawhirimātea runs out of puff,
and no windmills turn, and no sails arc,
and the Province of O's becalmed, floating in the dark.

Mātāriki from Takarunga, Devonport

23 June 2009

Auckland's monster brain, even asleep, pulses
with electric flashes: a live volcanic field –
urban magma, glowing, larval, wormy,
while Skytower blazes like a firebrand to flush
out werewolves, except there's no moon beaming,
just a black vault thick with glitter, celestial
frost wheeling above the summit of Takarunga,
Mount Victoria, eighty-one metres above the harbour;
and I've walked its spiralling road in the dark to keep
a vigil, be a stargazer, a look-out posted in the prow
of a waka, scanning the skies for Mātāriki's eyes.

I lie on my back against the lip of the crater,
to gaze up like an anti-gravity bungee-jumper
at the star-trek of spaceship Earth in bigger-
than-Imax glory, with 360 degree sensurround;
am gathered into spiral arms of the Milky Way;
then for a moment feel light-years from home –
consciously amid the cosmic laboratory a specimen –
and the closed throat of the vent below me hums.
It might be a hangar where raupo kites are stored
that can duel with the hawk, whose cold plumes
coast without lull from Ruapehu or Ngauruhoe.

Hill leviathan, fit for temple or observatory,
this scoria lump, pitted and terraced, once wore
a cloak woven of fern, bracken, flax, manuka;
then was a site for palisades, stratagems, ambuscades,
flag-raisings; for signal masts, cannon to warn foes
emphatic as war god Tumatauenga's stuck-out tongue.
Now I stalk across its carpark a nocturnal weka,
looking towards Rangitoto, Tiritiri, Tikapa Moana,
below Maui's fishhook, the anchor of the Great Waka,
the moko of some mighty face streaked with stardust –
the wink of tiny eyes sparkling like lures of paua.

Go tell it on the mountain; let its green bell chime
above cemetery's melancholy, stoplights, roofs.
New tides of day roll in: Te Ra dyes the sea blue,
and floats of a fishing net form islands in the Gulf.
All is flux: shadows boiling; a mad whirl of gulls
chasing ferry's backwash as it departs for the underworld.
Trypot's bubbling anchorage is a cauldron of dolphins
surfacing, or black-shelled mussels steaming in a kitchen.
Curtains go back on a villa window, and a behemoth
glides to the container port like a horizontal skyscraper,
orange as ripe persimmons in winter's leafless orchard.

Winebar Waiata

Significant others cry out to the land as mother.
Some confess to a feeling for forest.
Everyone nurtures small fantasies of doing a good job.
Everyone is a troubled spirit bailing away,
wanting the trappings of success.
Skipping lines of rain recede
in salt, vinegar, mustard, pepper rainbows.
Sleep of kiwis brings forth Mansfields and Frames.
Pine trees grow cardboard for toothpaste tubes.
But what becomes of the Mongrel Mob?
And how far can we push on
before we have to push back?
And where have all the father-figures gone?
The sun, caught on barbed wire, bleeds.

Kaiwhakaani, the Ventriloquist

I levelled hills for cycleways and walks;
spaded my birthday cake with twisted fork;

clashed over water on the chessboard plain;
and made navigators of the great canoes

exchange their mats for crisp white boat shoes.
I joined a debt queue, by rot-gut fortified;

pitched my tent amidst industrial blight.
Danced the Roaring Forties in gumboot tango;

chomped on mutton fat; gulped beer for smoko;
baled the mob up tightly with binder twine.

With weasel's tunnel vision, watched as godwits
trooped down the aisles of jumbo jets.

I sacrificed forests for the sake of toothpicks,
then played dead for a hundred years,

until the war between ourselves was settled
by a game of knucklebones using the Treaty's fist.

Taranaki Bitter

Bitter rain barnstorms green's mean ark,
bringing a hairy eyeball to play on
the velocity of culture vultures, who talk
in offal accents of their new dreamland,
where it's the zeal of gods rolling their own
that is slapped down amidst hilliness,
ocean horizon's long grab at nothing.

Shearers wrestle sodden sheep off ute trays.
Lizards of steam climb the kitchen ceiling.
Lather's not strained as each glass is drained.
Choruses of bubbly streams traverse gullies
to echo the roar of a river's welcome,
while solitude of rain gangs up on all
gathered at Queen Tuatara's funeral.

Heraldry

Hand upraised beneath a cloak of mist;
the colonial goose is cooked and eaten;
triple-chinned wonders soak in hot springs,
while seals bask on Zealandia's sundeck.

Loneliest place on loneliest planet,
where quilting bees sew pastures silver,
dairy queen udders from snowy alps burst,
and cast-off pine cones await collection.

Dip your toe in Marlborough wine lakes;
dodge falls of rock climbers out of mountains;
read the grain of a given piece of timber;
wad cardboard into rugby ball shapes.

Blood sport jokers jockey for lunch money;
tractor blockades smoke the Beehive out;
pre-mixed under-agers gatecrash winebars;
blat of grrrl racers burls down boulevards.

Fox Glacier launches a hot fridge brand;
fine wool clouds gather fattened lambs;
paddock barbed wire's bent round in a crown;
urgent hayseeds gee up Race Cup steeds.

A name that ripples in red, white, blue;
a slippery pill popped from a seething scrum,
half freezer pack, half frozen shoulder;
ref's whistle to raffle off a brassy win.

Weet-Bix bards at breakfast address their mums;
hip-hop stutters through blizzards of abuse;
snowboarding bohunks neck ekkies with glee;
all eyes on screens fix, held by glue.

Twenty Second Century

I remember it as it was, smells that rushed you,
raindrops in rings on deep river water,
the last shrivelled brown petal of summer,
wizened quinces cradled in earthen bowls,
a chrysalis dusted with frost's glitter,
newborns wobbling to cop bush justice
in freezing works, those spectres of meat.
And the scrum of bones flung from a pit
by archaeologists on a dig, old ladies
who stewed like possum tucker in wool coats,
mouldered stacks of *Listeners* germinating
a wilderness in back garden sheds.

Now keyboard workers as fascist playthings
sculpt muscles at Les Mills to a triumph
of the will, and scapegoats are sought
for dopamine feelgoods, while beauty
and her beast struggle on a luggage carousel
in a tv face-off watched by a demographic.
And Carlos Daze enjoys life in a Holden
rustbucket as an economic migrant
of the first water, searching by night
in second-hand shop bins for cast-offs,
homeless in a Middle Earth
being prepared for strip-mines by Orcs.

Notes on Poems

'Five Cent Coin' was written to commemorate the 2006 removal of
the New Zealand five cent coin from circulation. 'On Beauty' is a free
translation of a poem by Charles Baudelaire: La Beauté in *Fleurs du Mal*.
'Elvis and the Vulcans' was written as a response to the Iraq War several
years after its beginning in March 2003. 'Barnes Dance, Queen Street,
Auckland': The Barnes Dance is a method of crossing an intersection
diagonally, named after the American traffic engineer who designed
it, Henry Barnes, and adopted by the Auckland City Council in 1958.
This poem plays on the idea of the country and western barn dance, as
well as various kinds of street theatre and protest marches associated
with Queen Street over the years as the nation's premier commercial
thoroughfare. 'At Macraes Flat' is dedicated to Jill Dunwoodie (1931–
2008), and was written on the first anniversary of her death.
'Dada Dunedin' was originally commissioned for a project initiated by
Roel Wijland, exploring the marketing and 'branding' of Dunedin.

Acknowledgements

A Tingling Catch – A Century of NZ Cricket Poems 1864-2009; Blackmail
Press (on-line); *Coastlines*; *Crest to Crest – Impressions of Canterbury*; *Critic*,
Deep South (on-line); *The Dominion-Post*, *Dreadlocks*; *Home & Away* – a
Trans Tasman Symposium (on-line at nzepc); *International Literary Quarterly*
(on-line); *Jaam*, *Landfall*; *Lumiere Reader* (on-line); Mark Hutchins
Gallery (Wellington); Manawatu Festival of New Arts 2010; *Mauri
Ola – Contemporary Polynesian Poetry in English*; *New Zealand Books*, *New
Zealand Listener*, *New Zealand Poetry Society Anthology 2009 – Moments in the
Whirlwind*; *Otago Daily Times*; *Seven Stars – a Project for Matariki 2009* (on-
line at nzepc); *Side Stream*, *Takahe*; *The Press*; *Turbine 09* (on-line at nzetc).

A number of these poems were written or drafted while I was
Writer-in-Residence at the Michael King Writer's Centre in Devonport,
Auckland between April and June 2009.

Index of Poems